CW00781510

A North Wales Railway Travelogue

On 20th July 1964, *Merddin Emrys* passes Boston Lodge heading for Portmadoc.
The fireman on the right hand side of the engine is Peter Woods.

Frontispiece - Passing Minffordd on 12th August 1964, No. 10 *Merddin Emrys* heads for Tan-y-Bwlch on the Festiniog Railway with a morning train. The driver is Evan Davies.

A North Wales Railway Travelogue

Donald Peddie

Lightmoor Press

❀ *Contents* ❀

The HSBT Project team has kindly offered comments on certain aspects of locomotive details. For details of the HSBT Project, which aims to leave for future generations an authentic record of the fate of the 17,000 steam locomotives that existed in the last twelve years of the British Railways steam era, visit www.wrhts.co.uk

© Lightmoor Press and Donald Peddie 2014

Designed by Tony Miller; Cover design by Neil Parkhouse

British Library Cataloguing-in-Publication Data. A catalogue record for this book is available from the British Library

ISBN 9781899889 92 1

All rights reserved. No part of this publication may be reproduced, stored in a retrieval system or transmitted in any form or by any means, electronic, mechanical, photocopying, recording or otherwise, without the written permission of the publisher.

Lightmoor Press is an imprint of

Black Dwarf Lightmoor Publications Ltd

Unit 144B, Lydney Trading Estate, Harbour Road, Lydney, Gloucestershire GL15 4EJ

info@lightmoor.co.uk / www.lightmoor.co.uk

Printed and bound by Berforts Information Press Ltd, Eynsham, Oxford

❦ *Introduction* ❦

If my late father, Ian Peddie (1913-2006), had one abiding passion, in addition to that for Scottish railways, it was for the narrow gauge lines of North Wales. He photographed the Scottish railway scene from 1947 to the end of steam traction in 1967, and having compiled two volumes of his work in that respect, friends who knew of his Welsh railway interest and the photographs he took there in the 1954 to 1965 period, suggested I should draw these together into a further publication. Hence this volume, which will serve not only as a record of his work but will also hopefully give some overview of the early days of Welsh narrow gauge railway preservation, together with an appreciation of some other lines, which were still commercially operational.

Of course, standard gauge lines were never far away from visits to the narrow gauge scene and having a Scottish Region lineside photographic pass, it was not too difficult to make suitable arrangements to visit locomotive depots such as Llandudno Junction, Aberystwyth, Machynlleth and others as circumstances arose. The weather of course could never be guaranteed, though the Western Region locomotives were very different from those seen in Scotland, so there was the appeal of the new and unusual to stimulate his interest.

Without exception, the images in this volume were taken whilst on family holidays in Wales, which ranged from the North Wales coast resorts to

Ian Peddie at Aviemore in the 1980s

those on Cardigan Bay, a number of holidays being taken at several locations over the twelve year period. At my father's insistence, hotels were used in the localities, giving my mother a complete break for two or three weeks from her normal routine, something she much appreciated. However, coming from a railway family, she could not quite see what the excitement of the narrow gauge scene was all about and a degree of forbearance was needed as father pursued his interests. The holidays were, naturally, long remembered as outstanding successes.

As a lifelong engineer, though not a railway employee, my father was never happier than when in a locomotive works or engine shed, talking of pertinent technical matters with those around him. Not for him the pull of the glamorous and fast express locomotives, he being more inclined towards the unusual and the elderly locomotives and rolling stock.

As a time served engineer, who had worked through the late 1920s and early 1930s depression, he had empathy with those working 'on the tools'.

As one might expect, he kept accurate and comprehensive notes covering all his railway photographic images, the Welsh material being no exception, the notes being prepared immediately the respective images were secured. Indeed, there is a 1957 Valentine's postcard of Towyn Wharf station, taken from the overbridge, which depicts him making notes having recorded *Talyllyn* and its train. His notebooks are a unique record of his work and I have drawn upon them extensively for this publication.

The inclusion of a representative selection of standard gauge images, especially where some of the locations, such as Afon Wen Junction, have disappeared from the railway map, serve as a reminder of the 1960s rail closures, usually ascribed to Dr Beeching, though actively endorsed by an acquiescent railway management under political direction. If the current parliamentary structure governing Wales had been in place in the early 1960s, some important elements of the lost network might well have been saved but the damage was done.

Much has changed in the fifty plus years since the majority of images were taken, this being particularly so in the various narrow gauge locomotive workshops, where, at Boston Lodge, Coed-y-Park, Pendre and elsewhere, unguarded belt driven machinery was then in daily use. Additionally, on the Talyllyn Railway, the company was exempt from railway regulations requiring the use of continuous brakes throughout the train. Workshop facilities were then much more rudimentary, the main objective on the preserved lines being to keep the railway operational, sometimes on a day-to-day basis. The building of new narrow gauge locomotives in modern well equipped workshops was, in the mid-1950s, beyond the wildest dreams of the most optimistic enthusiast.

I am grateful to Lightmoor Publications for their support and encouragement with this project. Any errors in photographic captions can be laid squarely on the content of my father's notebooks, for which I take full responsibility.

Donald Peddie
Blanefield 2013

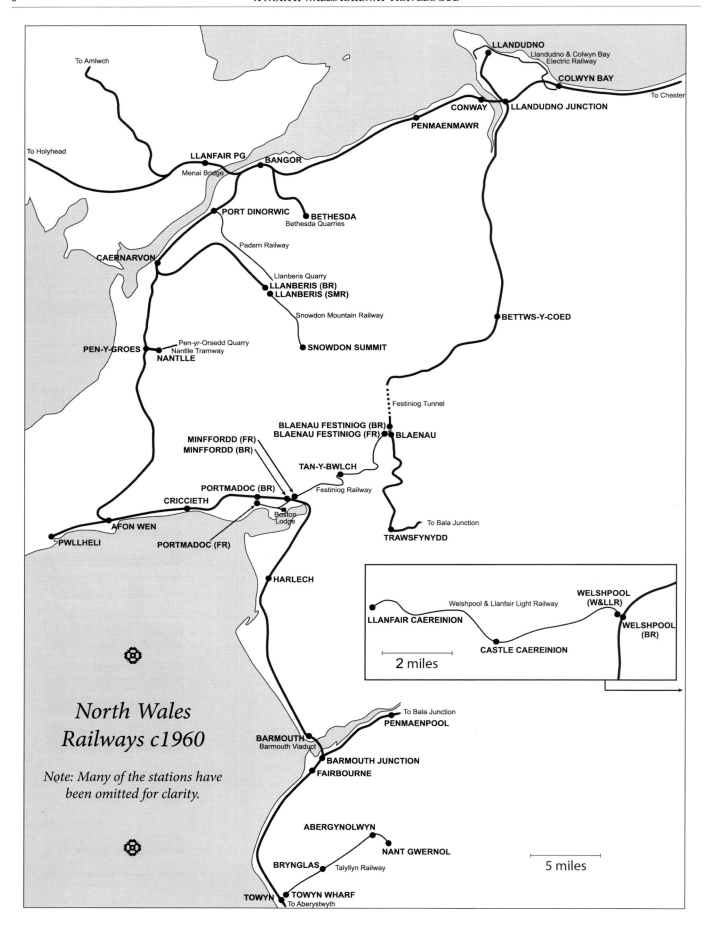

To Amlwch

To Holyhead

LLANDUDNO

Llandudno & Colwyn Bay
Electric Railway

COLWYN BAY

To Chester

CONWAY

LLANDUDNO JUNCTION

PENMAENMAWR

LLANFAIR PG

BANGOR

Menai Bridge

PORT DINORWIC

BETHESDA

Bethesda Quarries

Padarn Railway

CAERNARVON

Llanberis Quarry

LLANBERIS (BR)
LLANBERIS (SMR)

Snowdon Mountain Railway

BETTWS-Y-COED

Pen-yr-Orsedd Quarry
Nantlle Tramway

PEN-Y-GROES

NANTLLE

SNOWDON SUMMIT

Festiniog Tunnel

BLAENAU FESTINIOG (BR)
BLAENAU FESTINIOG (FR)

BLAENAU

MINFFORDD (FR)
MINFFORDD (BR)

TAN-Y-BWLCH

PORTMADOC (BR)

Festiniog Railway

CRICCIETH

Boston
Lodge

AFON WEN

To Bala Junction

PWLLHELI

PORTMADOC (FR)

TRAWSFYNYDD

HARLECH

WELSHPOOL
(W&LLR)

Welshpool & Llanfair Light Railway

LLANFAIR CAEREINION

WELSHPOOL
(BR)

2 miles

CASTLE CAEREINION

To Bala Junction

PENMAENPOOL

*North Wales
Railways c1960*

BARMOUTH

Barmouth Viaduct

BARMOUTH JUNCTION

FAIRBOURNE

*Note: Many of the stations have
been omitted for clarity.*

ABERGYNOLWYN

NANT GWERNOL

BRYNGLAS

Talyllyn Railway

5 miles

TOWYN

TOWYN WHARF

To Aberystwyth

❀ *Llandudno Junction - British Railways* ❀

Passenger traffic destined for the North Wales coastal resorts resulted in Llandudno Junction hosting a variety of motive power in the holiday seasons. Moreover, the normal through passenger and freight services had to be catered for, as well as the need to provide power for local branch line services, which in the early 1960s were still significant in the North Wales area: quarried stone and other bulk freight traffic was also dealt with. In the 1962 and 1963 summer holiday periods, Llandudno Junction depot was visited several times.

Plate 1 – Locally based BR 'Britannia' 7MT No. 70017 *Arrow*, built at Crewe in 1951, simmers between duties on 3rd July 1963. Originally allocated to the Western Region, this engine has hand holds on the smoke deflectors, which replaced the original handrails following the Milton accident of November 1955, involving No. 70026 *Polar Star*. It was claimed that this accident, involving fatalities, resulted because signal sightings were obstructed by the smoke deflector handrails. In August 1966, whilst allocated to Kingmoor, No. 70017 was damaged by running into a freight train at Carlisle when heading a southbound empty stock train. The locomotive was subsequently withdrawn and cut up by J. Cashmore at Newport.

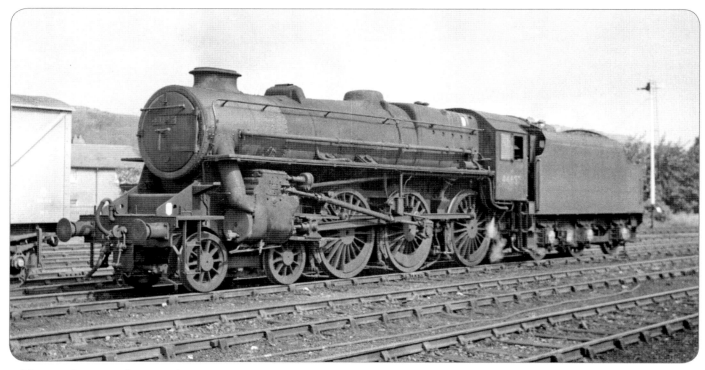

Plate 2 – Caprotti valve geared 5MT No. 44687, built with a high running plate and double chimney, was in light steam between duties at Llandudno Junction on a sunny 1st July 1963. Built at Horwich in 1951, and reputedly a most successful design in all respects, it is difficult to understand why this type was not replicated in large numbers, rather than the production of a completely new standard class 5MT. No. 44687's valve gear was driven through two outside drive shafts, and the engine was fitted with SKF roller-bearing axle boxes. Unfortunately, No. 44687 would be withdrawn in January 1966 from Southport, and was scrapped by J. Cashmore at Great Bridge a few months later.

✿

Plate 3 – Push-pull fitted LM&SR designed '2MT' tank engine No. 41220 was photographed at Llandudno on 29th June 1963 awaiting its next turn. Carrying a 6C shedplate, and built by BR at Crewe in 1948, this engine would outlive many of the BR-designed standard Class '2MT' tanks, which again questions the decision to design a new standard Class '2MT' tank engine rather than replicate the existing LM&SR type. No. 41220 was withdrawn from Stockport in November 1966 and scrapped by J. Cashmore at Great Bridge.

Plate 4 – Taking water on 8th July 1963, ex-LM&SR Class '3FT' No. 47669 was typical of the locomotives used for local goods trip work and yard shunting in the North Wales area. Built at Horwich in 1931 this engine, along with many of its sisters, would be swept away through a decline in freight traffic and the wholesale introduction of 350hp diesel shunting engines. Withdrawn from Llandudno Junction in 1965, No. 47669 was scrapped by T.W. Ward at Sheffield.

Plate 5 (below) – Built by BR at Crewe in 1948, Caprotti valve geared '5MT' No. 44738 was also in light steam at Llandudno on 3rd July 1963. No. 44738 was the first of a batch of ten locomotives built with Caprotti valve gear, the LM&SR intention being to compare performance with the normal Walschaerts' arrangement. To accommodate this valve gear, the boiler pitch was raised by two inches from the standard arrangement and the chimney set forward on an extended smokebox. To provide room for the big cannon-type axleboxes the standard 7ft + 8ft coupled wheel spacing was modified, the latter figure being increased to 8ft 4ins. The valve gear was driven through a single central inside drive from the leading coupled axle and, as with all LM&SR-designed Caprotti '5MT's, the cab and front steps were of the open plate variety. A practical working defect of this LM&SR arrangement was that these engines could not be reversed directly from or to an intermediate cut-off position, but had first to be moved to the full-gear position in the new direction required. No. 44738 had one more year of revenue earning service, before being withdrawn from Speke Junction in 1964 and scrapped at BR Crewe.

Plate 6 – Crewe North based '7MT' No. 70000 *Britannia*, having worked a special from the south, was being serviced at Llandudno on 7th July 1963. As with a number of this class, the original smoke deflector handrails have been replaced with hand holes. This view also shows that *Britannia* had been fitted with a speedometer, there being a crank on the rear left hand coupled wheel and the associated drive to the cab. Built at Crewe in 1950 and originally allocated to Stratford, No. 70000 was withdrawn from Newton Heath in June 1966 and is preserved.

❁

Plate 7 – In light steam at Llandudno on 9th July 1963 was '8F' No. 48253, which had been built by the North British Locomotive Co. at Hyde Park Works, Glasgow, for the Ministry of Supply in July 1941 and shipped to Persia in November 1941. Originally WD No. 376, this '8F' had been bought by BR in 1949 and repatriated from Egypt. When photographed, No. 48253 was allocated to Mold Junction and was to be one of the last steam locomotives in service on BR, being withdrawn from Lostock Hall in August 1968. This shows the locomotive's left side, indicating that, as with early LM&SR and WD orders, a curved reversing rod was fitted.

Plate 8 – During the Second World War, the Ministry of Supply placed significant orders with the NB Locomotive Co., Glasgow, for Stanier '8F's on behalf of the War Department. One such was No. 48259, originally numbered 504 in the WD series, and shipped to Persia in November 1941. Dumped in Egypt post war, the engine was bought by BR in December 1949 and repatriated to the UK. Built in October 1941 at Hyde Park Works, No. 48259 was also in light steam at Llandudno on 9th July 1963 and would survive for a further two years until withdrawal from Mold Junction in July 1965. This view shows the right side, the Westinghouse air pump initially supplied being fitted to the smokebox on this side. Additionally, a star painted below the cab number indicates the locomotive was fitted with 50% reciprocating balance and suitable for fast freight and passenger work. No. 48259 was fitted with AWS in 1960, although appears to have lost its fore end vacuum standpipe.

Plate 9 – Holyhead based (6J), push-pull fitted standard class '2MT' tank No. 84001 was resting at Llandudno between duties on 29th June 1963. Used on local branch line passenger services, No. 84001 was built at Crewe in 1953 and withdrawn from Llandudno Junction in October 1964. Subsequently, the locomotive was scrapped at North Blyth in January of the following year.

Plate 10 – On 2nd July 1964, ex-LM&SR Class '7P' No. 46155 *The Lancer* rests between duties at the depot. A Crewe North engine at the time, No. 46155 was built at Derby in 1930 and rebuilt with a 2A boiler in 1950. Withdrawn from Carlisle Kingmoor in 1964, *The Lancer* was scrapped by Arnott Young at Troon in February 1965.

Plate 11 – Looking rather unkempt, locally based BR standard Class '2MT' tank No. 84020 awaits its next turn of duty on 2nd July 1963. Built at Darlington in 1957 and only six years old when captured at the depot, No. 84020 would survive for just over a year. The engine was withdrawn in October 1964 and scrapped at North Blyth in January of the following year, after less than eight years of revenue earning service. Like many examples of the '2MT' tank engine classes, No. 84020 would succumb to a combination of branch line closures and the introduction of diesel multiple units.

Plate 12 – On 3rd July 1963, 'Jubilee' Class '6P' No. 45610 *Ghana*, a visitor from Burton, was at rest in the depot. Built at Crewe in 1934, No. 45610 was originally named *Gold Coast* but was renamed in December 1958 when Ghana gained independence from the United Kingdom. Withdrawn from Derby in January 1964, *Ghana* was cut up at its birthplace. Adjacent to the 'Jubilee' Class engine is ex-LM&SR '5MT' No. 45277, which had worked a relief holiday special from the Midlands.

Plate 13 – BR Standard Class '9F' No. 92058 waits for the right away at Llandudno on 27th June 1962. In very clean condition, No. 92058 was built at Crewe in 1955. After only twelve years service this locomotive was withdrawn from Carlisle Kingmoor in November 1967 and scrapped by J. McWilliam at Shettleston, Glasgow, in February of the following year.

Plate 14 – Locally-based Stanier '8F' No. 48771 was in fact built at Doncaster Works in 1946, as a member of the L&NER's 'O6' Class. Initially numbered 3166 and subsequently 3566 by the L&NER, the locomotive was renumbered 8771 by the LM&SR in late 1947 on transfer to the latter company. When captured on 2nd July 1963, the engine was being prepared at Llandudno for a boiler wash out. No. 48771 was transferred to Lostock Hall, from where it was withdrawn in December 1965 and scrapped at Wigan the following year. In common with all '8F' wartime production, No. 48771 was built with shorter connecting rods, plus lengthened piston rods and union links, compared to the original pre-war design. Moreover, as with all latter wartime production locomotives, a straight reversing rod is fitted.

Plate 15 – A stranger to Llandudno Junction, ex-L&NER 'B1' Class No. 61104, which had worked a holiday special from the Midlands, was in light steam on 9th July 1963. Based at Canklow, No. 61104 had been in store over the 1962-63 winter period but was then pressed into service for holiday and excursion duties. This engine was built by North British Locomotive Co. at Glasgow in 1946 and had only one more year's service prior to withdrawal in April 1964. The Stones electric lighting generator, originally fitted to the right hand running board adjacent to the smokebox, had been removed by this time. The locomotive was scrapped by W.F. Smith at Ecclesfield later in that year.

Plate 16 – Locally based Caprotti valve geared '5MT' No. 44686 was at rest between turns at Llandudno on 3rd July 1963. Sister to No. 44687, and built by BR at Horwich in 1951, with high running plate and double chimney, No. 44686 was withdrawn from Southport in October 1965. This engine had the increased boiler pitch and enhanced coupled wheel spacing common to all the Caprotti valved locomotives. A possible preservation of this engine was considered but it was despatched for scrap to T.W. Ward at Beighton in January 1966.

Plate 17 – The MR/LM&SR Class '4F' 0-6-0, with its 5ft 3ins diameter wheels, was in reality a mixed traffic locomotive to be found on both passenger and freight workings throughout the LM&SR network. Numbering 772 engines, the class had been built at Derby, Crewe, St. Rollox and Horwich railway workshops, as well as by private builders including the North British, Kerr, Stuart and Barclay companies. On 12th July 1963, '4F' No. 44525 was engaged in shunting duties at Llandudno. Built at Crewe in 1928, No. 44525 was withdrawn in October 1966 and was the last of the class to remain in service, her final duties being as works shunter at Crewe, a task she shared with fellow '4F' No. 44405, this latter locomotive being withdrawn in June 1966. No. 44525 was despatched for scrap to Drapers of Hull in January 1967.

✿

Plate 18 – Carrying a 6C shed plate, standard Class '2MT' tank No. 84009 was resting between turns at Llandudno on 29th June 1963 and needing some attention to the superficial damage to the left hand valve chest cover and platework. Built at Crewe in 1953, No. 84009 was withdrawn in November 1965 and scrapped the following year, the engine having been 'stored serviceable' over the winter of 1963-64. Behind No. 84009 is one of the equivalent LM&SR designed '2MT' tanks, which is push-pull fitted.

❁ *De Winton Locomotives* ❁

The de Winton Company, having its origins in the 1840s in Caernarvon, built steam locomotives and quarry equipment until its failure in early Edwardian times. The company was a major supplier to the Welsh slate and stone quarrying industries, including the Penrhyn Quarries, the Pen-yr-Orsedd Quarry and the Penmaenmawr & Welsh Granite Co. Few of these original de Winton engines survive, the majority having been withdrawn prior to the Second World War.

Plate 19 – One of the surviving de Winton vertical boilered locomotives which worked at the Penrhyn Quarries was cosmetically restored and is preserved in the narrow gauge railway museum at Towyn. This photograph was taken in the original museum on 22nd July 1959, and shows 0-4-0 *George Henry*, which was built at Caernarvon and delivered to Penrhyn Quarries in May 1877. *George Henry* was active in the quarry until 1944 and is virtually complete, though inoperable.

Plate 20 – A second de Winton, similar to *George Henry* and initially named *Katie* (later *Kathleen*), was delivered to Penrhyn Quarries in June 1877 and this locomotive also worked until the mid-1940s. The incomplete remains of the engine were captured in the scrap line at Coed-y-Parc on the 27th June 1964. Happily, what in 1964 looked a wreck was subsequently acquired for preservation.

❀ *Welshpool & Llanfair Light Railway* ❀

Built to 2ft 6ins gauge and opened in 1903 to connect Welshpool with Llanfair Caereinion, the W&LLR was grouped with the GWR in 1923. Passenger services were discontinued in 1931 and the last BR goods train ran in November 1956. The line was initially leased from BR by the W&LLR preservation society in 1962, prior to outright purchase in 1974, passenger trains having restarted in April 1963. The line, unfortunately, no longer terminates in the centre of Welshpool, that part from Raven Square (the present terminus) to the original terminus being acquired by the local authority for a road development.

Plate 21 – Locomotive No. 1 *The Earl*, built by Beyer, Peacock at Manchester in 1902, is being serviced on a dull 26th August 1965 at Llanfair. Numbered 822 by the GWR, the Swindon 1925 rebuild influence on replacement locomotive fittings is obvious: the copper capped chimney, the dome cover form, the brass safety valve casing and the two whistles. No. 822 operated the last trains in BR days and, together with sister engine No. 823, was stored at Oswestry Works until secured by the W&LLR preservation company. In addition to the normal vacuum brake for train working, the locomotive is fitted with buffer beam mounted safety chains. Previously fitted carriage heating equipment had been removed by the mid-1950s.

The station yard at Llanfair on the same day contained items of rolling stock and locomotive No. 1. The original W&LLR bogie coaches, provided by R.Y. Pickering of Wishaw, Scotland, had been removed to Swindon in 1931 on cessation of the passenger service, and scrapped thereafter. In the upper photograph *(Plate 22)*, the coach directly behind the bogie mineral wagon is one of the 'toastrack' coaches acquired from the admiralty in 1961 and rebuilt as a closed carriage. Coupled behind it is 4-wheeled brake van No. 213, again rebuilt from an ex-Admiralty van. The lower photograph *(Plate 23)* shows a train of ex-Admiralty bogie coaches as running in 1965. Happily, replicas of the original bogie coaches have been built and are now in operation.

❀ *Dinorwic Quarry Railway* ❀

For some reason, fewer visits were made to the Dinorwic Quarry Railways plus the associated Padarn Railway and Port Dinorwic harbour. This may have been related to access difficulties to the works at Llanberis and the discouragement of visitors.

Running from Llanberis down to Port Dinorwic, the Padarn Railway carried slate on a 4ft gauge line, which had been opened in 1843, the last train running in October 1961. The railway gauge in the quarry itself and at Port Dinorwic harbour was 1ft 11ins.

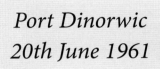

*Port Dinorwic
20th June 1961*

Plates 24 (above) and 25 – At Port Dinorwic, Hunslet No. 1429, built at Leeds in 1922, was shunting at the wharf although slate was being despatched by road. At this time, the locomotive was named *No. 1* but had previously carried the name *Lady Joan*. The port closed in late 1961, and *No. 1* then found work in the quarries until withdrawal in 1967. The engine survives in preservation at the Bredgar & Wormshill Railway.

Plate 26 – This view of the 4ft gauge Padarn Railway intermediate station at Pen-y-Llyn, looking towards Llanberis on 17th July 1961, shows a well maintained track and station platform. The siding diverging to the right was at one time used as a carriage siding for workmen's trains.

Plate 27 - The un-braked slate wagons in use at Port Dinorwic had double flanged wheels and the point work, as shown in this photograph, slewed both rails. To cross the BR standard gauge siding at the port, temporary narrow gauge track was laid across the BR track. To assist the weighing of finished slate, each wagon carried its tare weight on the solebar. Little remains today of these wharf facilities.

❀ 'Twixt Pwllheli and Criccieth – British Railways ❀

Several summer holidays were spent in the Criccieth district during the early 1960s and the opportunity was taken to visit local stations and depots to capture the various ex-GWR, ex-LM&SR and BR 'Standard' Class locomotives operating there at that time. There was then a connection from the ex-GWR Cambrian coast line to the former LM&SR Welsh coast route, which ran north from Afon Wen Junction, and which was used by both passenger and freight traffic.

Plate 30 – At Afon Wen station on 20th July 1962, a smartly turned out Llandudno Junction-based BR '4MT', No. 75010, awaits the signal before departure with a Pwllheli to Llandudno passenger working, a rail route which is no longer available to travellers. Facing west, the train appears to be operating 'wrong line' but this is due to the need for reversal at Afon Wen, since the junction leading to the LM&SR North Wales line was trailing from Pwllheli. No. 75010, built at Swindon in 1951, was withdrawn from Carnforth in October 1967 after only sixteen years revenue earning service and scrapped by Motherwell Scrap & Machinery, Wishaw, in February 1968.

Plate 31 – On 23rd July 1962, locally based ex-GWR '2251' Class No. 3208 was on ballast train duties a mile east of Criccieth station. One of the later examples of this class and in very clean condition, No. 3208 was built at Swindon in 1947 and withdrawn from Machynlleth shed in May 1965, by which time Machynlleth was in London Midland Region territory.

Plate 32 – Resting in the relatively hospitable and clean surroundings of Pwllheli shed on 19th July 1961, BR '2MT' tank No. 82000 awaits its next turn. Locally based and in reasonably clean condition, No. 82000 was built at Swindon in 1952 and withdrawn from Patricroft in December 1966.

Plate 33 – At Afon Wen Junction on 27th July 1962, an ancient ex-GWR 4-wheeled coach was still in departmental service, eighty years after its initial building. The coach, numbered W24W, weighed 11 tons and was supported on a wheelbase of 17ft 0ins; overall length was given as 28ft 2ins and width as 8ft 1in. Built at Swindon in 1882, the coach side panelling was stencilled 'Oswestry MPD Tool Van'.

Plate 34 ≠ Heavy summer Saturday passenger traffic on the Cambrian coast line often required double heading leaving Pwllheli and here, on 22nd June 1960, BR '2MT' No. 78002 pilots ex-GWR 0-6-0 No. 3213 east of Criccieth on an eastbound train. Both locomotives are blowing off as they prepare for the climb to Black Rock, before running down into Portmadoc. The BR '2MT' would be withdrawn in 1966 after fourteen years service and No. 3213 in 1963, after sixteen years service.

Plate 35 - Ex-GWR '4300' Class No. 6395 was in the process of disposal at Pwllheli shed on 22nd June 1961; smokebox ash remains to be swept from the footplate and the smokebox door secured. Locally based No. 6395, which is fitted with GWR ATC equipment, was built by Robert Stephenson in 1921 and was withdrawn from Stourbridge shed in November 1964, after a creditable forty-three years service. Before the advent of BR 'Standard' locomotives, these ex-GWR moguls were the mainstay of Cambrian coast passenger services.

Plate 36 – Oswestry-based BR '4MT' No. 75050 draws into Criccieth station whilst bound for Pwllheli, with a passenger working on 17th July 1962. Built at Swindon in 1956, No. 75050 was withdrawn in 1966 after only ten years service.

Plate 37 – Locally based BR '4MT' No. 75020, with double chimney, rests under cover in the relatively modern and well kept locomotive shed at Pwllheli on 22nd July 1961. Built at Swindon in 1953, No. 75020 would be among the last BR operational steam locomotives when withdrawn from Carnforth in August 1968.

Plate 38 – On a sunny 20th July 1961, ex-GWR 2-6-0 No. 6392 leaves Criccieth on a passenger service from Pwllheli to the south. No. 6392 was retained for 1961 summer services but was withdrawn, after a forty year working life, in October 1961 and scrapped at Swindon.

Plate 39 – Afon Wen was the southern junction connection between the GWR Cambrian coast route and the LM&SR North Wales line. The route, which was most unfortunately lost through government cuts, ran north through Penygroes and Caernarvon, joining the LM&SR main line half a mile west of Treborth Hall. On 22nd July 1961, BR Class '4MT' No. 75026 waits at Afon Wen with a through passenger service for Bangor. Locally based, No. 75026 was built at Swindon in 1954 and was withdrawn from Tebay in December 1967, having had a double chimney fitted in 1962. Part of this lost route, between Dinas and Caernarvon, is now occupied by the resurrected Welsh Highland Railway.

Plate 40 – On 20th July 1962, BR Class '3MT' tank No. 82034 approaches Criccieth from the west with a local passenger working from Pwllheli. Built at Swindon in 1955, No. 82034 was withdrawn in December 1966.

❁

Plate 41 – At Criccieth station, BR-built '2MT' tank No. 41234 from Bangor shed waits to leave on a holiday relief working for the North Wales coast, on 21st July 1962. The route will be via Afon Wen Junction and Caernarvon. No. 41234, built at Crewe in 1949, was destined to be withdrawn from Sutton Oak in November 1966.

Plate 42 – At Criccieth in sunny conditions on 27th July 1962, locally based '3MT' tank engine No. 82009 is about to depart for Machynlleth on a passenger working from Pwllheli. Built at Swindon in 1952, No. 82009 would survive until 1966.

Plate 43 – At Pwllheli on 19th July 1961, a very clean BR '2MT' No. 78000 was parked at the back of the shed. Built at Darlington in 1952, locally based No. 78000 would be withdrawn from Derby in 1965.

Plate 44 – Stopped at Criccieth station awaiting clearance to proceed east on 27th July 1962, locally based BR '3MT' tank No. 82005 heads a Pwllheli to Machynlleth pick-up freight working. Built at Swindon in 1952, No. 82005 would remain in service until 1965, when it would be withdrawn from Nine Elms. At this time there was a significant amount of rail freight traffic in the area, since road links were not what they are today.

Plate 45 – In the same month, on 19th July 1962, ex-GWR '2251' Class No. 2268 was in light steam in the disposal road at Pwllheli shed. Like No. 2257 in *Plate 48*, it was built at Swindon in 1930. Again based locally, No. 2268 would survive another five years until withdrawal from Machynlleth in May 1965.

Plate 46 - On 21st July 1961, former GWR '4300' Class No. 7302 calls at Criccieth with an eastbound passenger working. Built by Robert Stephenson & Co. in 1921, No. 7302 was withdrawn in August 1962 from Pontypool Road.

Criccieth
July 1961

Plate 47 – Former GWR 'Mogul' 2-6-0 No. 6392 again, heading a local passenger working east of Criccieth on 23rd July 1961. This engine was built in 1921 by Robert Stephenson & Co.

Plate 48 – In the late 1950s, the mainstay of Cambrian coast services prior to the introduction of the BR 'Standard' classes rested with ex-GWR 2-6-0 and 0-6-0 classes, the 2-6-0 locomotives in particular being a most successful design. On 27th July 1962, ex-GWR '2251' Class No. 2257 was at rest at Pwllheli. Built at Swindon in 1930, No. 2257 was withdrawn from Reading in August 1964. Pwllheli, with its associated holiday camp, generated much holiday season passenger traffic and this engine retains its train reporting number on the upper smokebox lamp bracket, as well as showing the remains of that number chalked on the smokebox door.

Plate 49 – Also pictured on Pwllheli shed was ex-GWR 2-6-0 No. 7302 from Hereford. Built by Robert Stephenson in 1921, No. 7302 would survive for only another few weeks, being withdrawn from Pontypool Road in August 1962 after a respectable forty plus years of revenue earning service.

Narrow Gauge Railway Museum, Towyn

Located at the Towyn Wharf station of the Talyllyn Railway, adjacent to a BR standard gauge siding, the initial museum building was constructed in 1956, to house items which otherwise might have been lost to posterity. A new museum was opened in 2005, the photographs below being taken in the earlier building.

Plate 50 – Dot, an 18in. gauge 0-4-0WT, was built by Beyer, Peacock & Co. at Gorton Foundry, Manchester in 1887. It was used on the Lancashire & Yorkshire's Horwich Works narrow gauge railway for shunting and internal works movements. The locomotive was restored at Gorton in 1960 and arrived at the museum in 1961, where it was captured on 24th of July that year.

Plate 51 – Guiness Brewery 0-4-0T No. 13, whose design was patented by Samuel Geoghegan, was built by William Spence & Co. of Dublin in 1895, specifically to operate in the confines of the brewery at St. James' Gate, Dublin. Built to a gauge of 1ft 10ins, the locomotive operated there until 1951 and arrived at the museum in 1956. The engines and valve gear are mounted on top of the boiler, power being transmitted to the wheels via vertical connecting rods. No. 13 was photographed in the museum on 22nd July 1959.

Plate 52 – Cambrai, a French metre gauge locomotive fitted with outside Allen straight link motion, was built in Paris in 1888 for the Chemin de Fer du Cambresis and purchased in 1936 by the Loddington Ironstone Co. The engine later moved to Waltham Ironstone Quarries near Melton Mowbray. Presented to the museum in 1960, *Cambrai* was standing outside the museum on 24th July 1961. It is currently located on the Irchester Narrow Gauge Railway.

❀ *Welsh Highland Railway* ❀

The WHR was formed in 1922 through the grouping of two former and by then bankrupt railway companies, that had operated along parts of what was to become the WHR trackbed. The railway was abandoned in 1937 and the track lifted, as scrap, in 1941, to supply material for the war effort; most of the rolling stock was scrapped at that time. In the mid-to-late 1950s, who could have imagined that in the following fifty years the Welsh Highland Railway would be completely restored as a thriving operational railway. After all, the Festiniog Railway had only been operating as a preserved line for two or three years and few, if any, vestiges of the erstwhile Welsh Highland Railway then remained.

❀

Plate 53 – Through purchase by the Birmingham Locomotive Society the former WHR 2-6-2T *Russell* was saved in the mid-1950s and moved to the Talyllyn Railway at Towyn. Stored in the open at the back of the first narrow gauge museum adjacent to Wharf Station, *Russell* was in very rundown condition when pictured there on 19th July 1958. Built by Hunslet in 1906, the locomotive was named after J.C. Russell, the chairman of the North Wales Narrow Gauge Rly Co. Unusually, the engine had outside frames for the driving wheels and inside frames for the trailing and pony trucks, the latter lying detached in the foreground. When the WHR was dismantled in 1941, *Russell* was requisitioned for the war effort and subsequently sold to private industry, from which it was bought for preservation. Full restoration was completed in 1987.

❀

Plate 54 – Two former WHR bogie carriages, No's 26 and 23 (to the left), were in service at the FR's Harbour station, Portmadoc, on 18th July 1961. Both were built by the Ashbury Carriage & Wagon Co. of Manchester for the North Wales Narrow Gauge Railway in 1894 and passed into WHR stock in 1922. No. 26 was sold by the WHR demolition contractor in 1942 to a farmer for use as a henhouse but was acquired by the Festiniog Railway in 1959 and rebuilt. No. 23 was acquired from the WHR by the Festiniog Railway in 1936 and was used in 1955 on the first train to leave Portmadoc in the preservation era. Both carriages have subsequently been rebuilt.

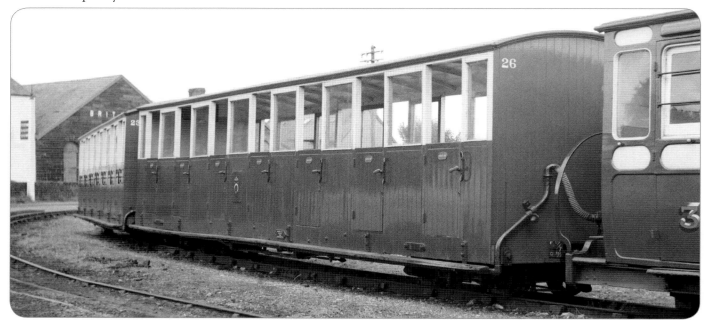

❀ *Llandudno & Colwyn Bay Electric Railway Ltd* ❀

Built in various stages between 1907 and 1915, this 3ft 6ins gauge electric tramway operated between these two North Wales seaside resorts until 1956. The lines, which were mainly double track from 1929, ran through the streets of the towns through which the company operated. It was extremely popular with tourists, despite intense competition from Crossville buses (operated by the GWR/BR). The L&CBER converted to motor bus operation in 1956 but the company was bought out by Crossville (then nationalised) and ceased independent operation in 1961. One tramcar survived, No. 6, originally built in 1914 for Bournemouth Corporation, and until 1974 it was displayed at the BTC museum at Clapham. It later returned to Bournemouth and was restored to No. 85, its number when operating on the south coast.

Plate 55 – On 4th August 1954, L&CBER single-deck open 'toastrack' bogie car No. 19 makes its way past Little Orme on the way to Llandudno Pier. The sixty-seat car is filled with holidaymakers and it seems there is standing room only. The tram bodies were provided in 1933 by the United Electric Car Co., the bogies and traction control equipment coming from English Electric. No. 19 and its three sister cars were withdrawn in 1956, when electric tramway operation ceased.

Plate 56 – At the same location and on the same day in 1954, car No. 13 also makes its way to Llandudno Pier. This open-top, double-decked bogie car was originally built for Bournemouth Corporation, being acquired by the L&CBER second-hand in 1936 as part of a block purchase of ten such vehicles. On these trams, the bogies and traction control equipment had been provided by Brill/Brush. Car No. 13 was withdrawn in 1956 and it is one of this type which survives in preservation. The advertising board on the top deck pointing to Catlin's Follies is indicative of the entertainment enjoyed by holidaymakers of the period.

❀ *Festiniog Railway* ❀

Built to carry slate from the quarries around Blaenau Festiniog to Portmadoc, the railway was originally gravity and horse operated when opened in 1836. The railway closed in 1946 but reopened under preservation company ownership in 1954. By overcoming many major difficulties, the original terminus at Blaenau Festiniog was regained in 1982 and the railway is now a major undertaking and tourist attraction. Family visits were made to the FR between 1958 and 1964, usually during the respective holiday seasons.

Plate 57 – On a sunny 26th August 1962, the erstwhile *Taliesin*, now renamed *Earl of Merioneth*, runs round at Tan-y-Bwlch, the then FR northern terminus. This view shows the fireman's side of the engine.

Plate 58 – Not all holiday weather was favourable for photography, as evidenced by No. 2 *Prince* taking water and being serviced in the rain at Boston Lodge on 17th July 1962. Built by George England of South London in 1863, *Prince* was rebuilt at Boston Lodge in 1955.

Plate 59 – On 23rd July 1959, Fairlie type locomotive *Taliesin* was photographed at Harbour station. This engine was built at Boston Lodge works in 1885. Originally named *Livingston Thompson*, it was further renamed *Earl of Merioneth* in 1961. Withdrawn in 1971, the locomotive is now a static exhibit at the National Railway Museum, York. Coupled next to *Taliesin* is coach No. 23, a former Welsh Highland Railway bogie carriage built in 1894 and acquired by the FR in 1936.

Plate 60 – In 1961, a second Fairlie type returned to FR service. Built at Boston Lodge as No. 10 in 1879, *Merddin Emrys* had just re-entered traffic after a major overhaul. The locomotive was in red oxide primer paint and not completely fitted out when captured at Harbour station on 18th July 1961. No. 10 was one of the last two engines in service prior to FR closure in 1946.

Plate 61 (above) – On 20th July 1964, *Merddin Emrys* restarts a heavy train from Boston Lodge. The locomotive's fit-out is almost complete with spectacle plates and sand boxes in place. The driver, sporting his ever present cigarette, is Evan Davies.
Plate 62 (below) – *Taliesin*, recently renamed *Earl of Merioneth*, arrives at Harbour station on 10th July 1961.

Plate 63 (above) – In 1959 the Peddie family took a trip on the FR to Tan-y-Bwlch and on a sunny 8th July the party are seen in former WHR coach No. 26 at the then terminus. Note the Ashbury builder's plate in the corner. The train was hauled by *Taliesin* which is seen below *(Plate 64)* at the terminus prior to leaving for Portmadoc. The view shows the driver's side of the locomotive.

Plate 65 – The first steam locomotive to be used on the FR in 1863 was No. 1 *Princess* and it was also the last to be in service in August 1946, when the FR closed. To acknowledge the centenary of its construction, *Princess* was moved to Harbour station and is seen there on 12th July 1964. The engine is now displayed in a museum at Portmadoc.

Plate 66 – By 1964, sand boxes and spectacle plates had been fitted to *Merddin Emrys*. No. 10 and *Prince* rest after their respective daily duties during the evening of 10th August.

Plate 67 – In July 1962, the FR, being short of motive power, hired the Penrhyn Quarries Railway 0-4-0 *Linda* to support passenger services. By agreement with the owners, some modifications were made and the locomotive was also hired for the 1963 season, at the end of which it was purchased outright. Built by Hunslet at Leeds in 1893, *Linda* is seen working hard and making steady progress just north of Boston Lodge Halt on 20th July 1964.

In sylvan settings July 1964

Plate 68 – A fireman's eye view of the approach to the Cei Mawr stone embankment, as seen from the right hand footplate of *Linda* on 25th July 1964. This embankment is the longest natural stone structure on the line and possibly in the UK.

Plate 69 – Trains passing at Minffordd on 28th July 1964, as seen from the tender of the southbound train headed by ex-Penrhyn locomotive *Linda*. The guard of the stationary train from Portmadoc, headed by *Merddin Emrys*, is about to exchange staffs with the fireman of the southbound train. No. 10 has both blowers on to sustain boiler pressure for the climb to Tan-y-Bwlch.

Plate 70 - Having been impressed by the performance of *Linda*, the FR bought her sister engine *Blanche* in 1963. On 12th August 1964, *Blanche*, coupled to a small tender from one of the early FR 0-4-0s, awaits departure from Tan-y-Bwlch.

❁ *FR Termini* ❁

Plate 71 – At the Portmadoc terminus, the 3-way turnout at the west end of Harbour station remained in use for many years. This unusual arrangement, which was perhaps typical of slate railway track work and which has been replaced, was recorded on 18th July 1961.

❁

Plate 72 – The terminus of the FR line at Blaenau Festiniog was in a state of complete dereliction on 25th June 1961. By this time most of the removable scrap had been cleared, though the water tower remains in the middle distance. The scene is not helped by the dullness of the day and the overbearing mountains of slate from the Oakley Quarry. It would take more than twenty years endeavour against seemingly impossible odds, together with some major engineering works, before FR passenger trains returned to this location.

Plate 73 – During 1961, the overhauled *Merddin Emrys* was run-in prior to final outfitting and, on 22nd July, No. 10 is seen passing Boston Lodge heading for Tan-y-Bwlch, with a few steam leaks obvious. A series of boiler stay problems unfortunately limited the use of this engine and No. 10 was not in traffic again until 1963, having missed the entire 1962 season.

Plate 74 – The motive power shortage resulting from No. 10's unavailability was partially resolved by the purchase of the two Penrhyn Quarry engines and *Blanche* is seen here running round at Tan-y-Bwlch on 12th August 1964.

❀ *Boston Lodge* ❀

All repairs and servicing, together with rebuilding of locomotives and rolling stock, continues to be undertaken at Boston Lodge. Time spent there gave an interesting insight into the day by day activities essential to keep the railway running and of the dedicated operational staff at the core of these activities.

Plate 75 (above) – Usually used on permanent way and service trains, Baldwin 2-4-0 *Moelwyn* sits in the sun at Boston Lodge on 20th July 1960. Built as an 0-4-0 at Philadelphia in the USA in 1918 and acquired by the FR in 1925, *Moelwyn* was re-engined in 1956 and was occasionally pressed into assisting passenger train traffic. The engine had been vacuum fitted in 1928. The wagon coupled to *Moelwyn* is a 3-ton braked slate wagon, No. 249, used by the permanent-way gangers.

Plate 76 (right) - Even the usually reliable *Moelwyn* had her 'off days', as evidenced by Bob Harris examining a broken spring on 10th August 1964. With coupling and connecting rods removed, *Moelwyn* is placed over the wheel drop on the engine shed line adjacent to Glan-y-Mor yard

Plate 77 – On arrival from the Penrhyn Railway in July 1962, *Linda* was given a few trial runs prior to major modifications to meet FR requirements. These alterations included re-gauging, conversion to left-hand drive, fitting of a vacuum ejector and provision of a tender to increase coal and water capacity. Prior to these modifications being completed, *Linda* operated as a pilot engine on passenger trains, since no vacuum brake was then fitted. On 12th August 1962, *Linda* was parked at the back of the Boston Lodge shed line undergoing a piston and valve examination; the valve chest covers had been removed by Roger Goss. The engine is in 'as received' condition from Penrhyn Railway. Shortly after this date, *Linda* became derailed whilst piloting a passenger train and remained out of traffic until the re-gauging and brake enhancements were completed.

Plate 78 – The FR was always keen to acquire old rolling stock from other defunct narrow gauge railways and, in 1961, a bogie coach from the former Lynton & Barnstaple Railway was under reconstruction. Originally built in 1896 by the Bristol Carriage & Wagon Works, the coach underframe and bogies are shown on 26th July 1961, together with the various side panels which have been removed for refurbishment.

Plate 79 – Real progress in rebuilding the L&BR coach had been made in twelve months, as evidenced by this view taken in the works on 12th July 1962. The scene is also interesting since it shows the continued use of unguarded belt driven machinery, powered via overhead line shafts, plus significant propping of roof joists.

Rising like the phoenix – the Lynton & Barnstaple Railway coach

Plate 80 – The final result, buffet car No. 14, captured at Harbour station on 17th July 1963. It is amazing what can be achieved by a dedicated professional team over a two year period.

Plate 81 – Tucked away in Glan-y-Mor yard on a rainy 5th June 1963 were the remains of *Welsh Pony*, built for the FR by George England in 1867. The locomotive was last used in FR traffic in 1938, when a failed boiler hydraulic test resulted in it being set aside but it has now been cosmetically restored for display at Portmadoc.

❀

Plate 82 – More of a wreck than a locomotive, the remains of *Palmerston* continued to disintegrate in the undergrowth at Glan-y-Mor yard on 26th May 1961. Built as one of the original FR 0-4-0Ts by George England, *Palmerston* was withdrawn in 1940, and parts used for the rebuilding of *Prince* in 1955. These remains were not originally considered worthy of restoration, although in 1974 the remnants were privately purchased and the engine re-entered FR service in 1993 after restoration.

Plate 83 – Linda resting at Boston Lodge on 5th June 1963. The view shows the locomotive coupled to a 4-wheeled tender, reputedly from FR engine *Little Giant* and after the fitting of vacuum brake equipment. The combined train vacuum and engine steam brake controls are prominent at the driver's position on the left side of the cab. In fitting these braking arrangements, the locomotive was converted to left hand drive.

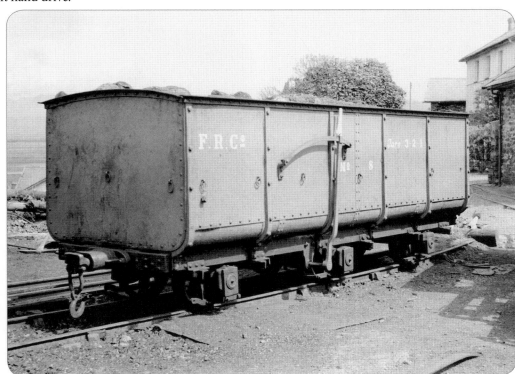

Plate 84 – Locomotive coal wagon No. 8 (tare weight 3tons 2cwts 1qtr – a good Imperial measure) fitted with a Cleminson 6-wheeled underframe, stands at Boston Lodge yard on 20th July 1961. With a carrying capacity of 8 tons, the wagon had been built at Boston Lodge in 1880 and was ultimately used for ash collection.

Plate 85 (above) – On 20th July 1964, the dismounted boiler from *Earl of Merioneth* and its top end bogie (*Plate 86 left*) are shown in the workshop, where the locomotive was undergoing major repairs. In 1971, *Earl of Merioneth* was taken out of service as its boiler was not economical to repair. The bottom end bogie from the withdrawn *Earl of Merioneth* was later substituted for that on *Merddin Emrys*, the bottom bogie on the latter engine having suffered an axle fracture in 1972.

❀ *FR Personalities* ❀

Plate 87 – The FR has always been blessed through the support of those whose professionalism and dedication enabled the railway to be the success that it continues to be. This scene shows (from the left), Peter Woods, Evan Davies and Findlay Binning at Boston Lodge on 23rd July 1964. *Merddin Emrys* has arrived on shed for disposal at the end of a hard day and there is much work still to do.

Plate 88 – Bill Hoole, on the driver's side of a spotlessly clean No. 10, prepares for his next turn, also in July 1964. Bill gave many years service to the FR, though not at line speeds operated by his previous employer. Bill joined the FR in mid-1959, on his retirement from BR service, with whom in May 1959, driving No. 60007 *Sir Nigel Gresley*, he established a post-war steam speed record of 112mph.

❁ *FR Rolling Stock* ❁

In the early years of preservation the FR operated with a range of rolling stock from a number of sources. Coaches running on the FR previously the property of the Welsh Highland Railway have been covered in the WHR section.

❁

Plate 89 – At Harbour station on 20th July 1959, coaches No's 22 (to the right) and 17 form part of a Portmadoc departure. No. 22 was built by the Ashbury Carriage & Wagon Co., Manchester, in 1896 and, as can be seen, had a slight sag in the roof. It had been returned to traffic in 1958 having been restored in the early preservation era; it has subsequently been significantly rebuilt.

Plate 90 – Two years later, on 18th July 1961, coach No. 17, built by Brown, Marshalls & Co. of Birmingham in 1876 and looking in excellent condition, is coupled to ex-WHR No. 26 at Harbour station. For some reason the covers have been left off the inspection/service pits then in use at the station.

Plate 91 – Coach No. 15, standing at Harbour station on 27th June 1961, was built by Brown, Marshalls & Co., Birmingham, in 1872, with bogies and running gear by Boston Lodge. Reputedly the first bogie carriage to enter revenue earning service on any British railway, and certainly the oldest in existence, No. 15 has subsequently been restored to Victorian splendour.

Plate 92 – FR carriage No. 10 is being given attention in the overgrown Glan-y-Mor yard on 23rd July 1961. The body was built by Brown, Marshalls & Co. of Birmingham in 1873, with bogies and running gear provided by Boston Lodge. In the early preservation era, van No. 10 had been used on many of the line clearance trains before falling into disuse in the late 1950s. Thoughts had been given to selling the vehicle, without the bogies. However, it was ultimately decided to retain and refurbish the carriage, which re-entered traffic in 1992.

Plate 93 – Standing in front of *Prince* at Boston Lodge on 23rd July 1962 are two ex-Croesor Tramway solid sided wagons. Numbered 51 and 52, they were acquired by the FR in the mid-1950s and were used for locomotive ash disposal. They were transferred to the Bala Lake Railway in the mid-1970s.

Plates 94 and 95 – Coaches No's 11 (*above*) and 12 (*below*), standing at Harbour station on 12th August 1964, were originally built as bogie luggage/brake vans by the Gloucester Railway Carriage & Wagon Co. in 1880, with no passenger accommodation. No. 11 was rebuilt as a passenger/brake vehicle at Boston Lodge with a new body in 1929 and was one of the first two carriages to be restored in the preservation era. Converted to a First class observation car in 1958 and provided with a steel underframe in 1962, the view shows the vehicle in that condition, painted in a green and ivory livery. No. 12 was similarly rebuilt at Boston Lodge in 1930 and restored in 1955, a buffet facility being added in 1957 and a steel underframe in 1963.

Plate 96 – Outside the former Boston Lodge engine shed on 23rd August 1962, an ex-Welshpool & Llanfair Light Railway cattle truck body rests on FR wagon body No. 461. This cattle truck, built by the GWR at Swindon in 1923 (as GWR No. 38089) for the Vale of Rheidol Railway, lay unused at Aberystwyth for many years. It was re-gauged by the GWR and sent to the W&LLR in 1937 then, in 1959, it was subsequently sold by BR to the FR. The body was shipped by rail from Welshpool to Minffordd in 1962 and the FR ultimately rebuilt it into a stores van of very changed appearance. Fortunately, from a heritage viewpoint, a similar GWR-built cattle truck, No. 38088, has survived in original form and has been fully restored by the W&LLR preservation society.

Plate 97 – Tucked away at the back of Boston Lodge works on 20th July 1961 was a 4-wheeled hearse van, complete with roof mounted wooden miniature Grecian urns, which reminds one of the all-encompassing nature of the Victorian railway business. Converted at Boston Lodge from a quarrymen's coach in 1883, the van was last used in the pre-preservation era in 1946. It was restored to running order in 1991 and is currently based at Gelert's Farm Works, Portmadoc. An assortment of metal fittings, including slate wagon wheels, rolling stock centre couplings and brake stands, provides an interesting forefront.

Plate 98 – Standing in the works yard on 10th August 1964 and designated as a cement carrier, is one of the original gunpowder vans built at Boston Lodge for firms supplying blasting powder to the quarries. The suppliers of the blasting powder reputedly owned these wagons, so in a sense they were private owner vehicles running on the FR. The body is of riveted construction with double doors at one end and is mounted on a standard slate wagon chassis. The van carries plate No. 16 and the internals would originally have been of wooden construction for powder storage.

Plate 99 – Brake van No. 2 was originally built as a quarrymen's carriage in the 1880s and was converted to a brake van at Boston Lodge around 1908, being fitted with a single balcony and vacuum brake. In the 1920s, it was additionally fitted with Westinghouse air brakes to allow operation on the WHR with their passenger stock. Rebuilt in 1958 with plywood body panels and removal of the Westinghouse equipment, the van was painted green and this view shows the vehicle in that condition on 5th June 1963, when in use as permanent way brake van. The vehicle has subsequently been further rebuilt.

Plate 100 – Goods brake van No. 1 stands in the Boston Lodge yard in July 1961. Formerly a quarrymen's carriage, it was re-bodied at Boston Lodge in 1908 with two balconies and formed part of the last pre-preservation era train in 1946. Following withdrawal in the mid-1960s, the remains were used as a shelter at Dduallt station until the early 1990s. The original vehicle no longer exists, although a replica was built in the 1990s.

Plate 101 – A group of 4-wheeled carriages await their next passengers at Harbour station on 12th August 1963. To the left, next to the brake van, is carriage No. 6 (number carried in 1963), built by Brown, Marshalls & Co. of Birmingham in 1864 and rebuilt at Boston Lodge in the 1880s as an open observation car. Restored in 1958 and renumbered 6, it was withdrawn in the mid-1960s and completely rebuilt to its original closed compartment condition. Many of the items introduced in the 1880s modifications were retained and incorporated in new carriage No. 1. The other three 4-wheeled vehicles are numbers 3, 4 and 5 and were supplied by the same builders in the same period, though none was modified in the same way as carriage No. 6.

❂ *FR Mishaps* ❂

Plate 102 – On 16th August 1962, *Earl of Merioneth* passes the entrance to Boston Lodge works with a return working to Harbour station.

Plate 103 – Captured north of Boston Lodge halt on 8th August 1964, *Merddin Emrys* and train slow down in preparation for stopping at the halt.

Plate 104 – On 25th July 1961, the first Harbour station departure, headed by *Merddin Emrys*, suffered a coach derailment just north of Bryn Halt, some three miles from Portmadoc. Passengers from the derailed train walked back to Bryn Halt, where *Prince* and *Moelwyn*, in top and tail mode, waited to take them back to Portmadoc. The view shows *Prince* waiting at Bryn Halt with passengers making their way to the relief train.

Plate 105 – During the running-in period in 1961-2, No. 10 *Merddin Emrys* was all too often to be found in the locomotive shed line adjacent to Glan-y-Mor yard. On 25th August 1962, No. 10 was stopped with leaking boiler stays, a faulty bottom bogie steam joint and damage to the left-hand cylinder drain cocks. As previously mentioned, the boiler staying problems kept the engine out of traffic for the rest of that season.

❀ *Pen-yr-Orsedd Quarry and Nantlle Tramway* ❀

The Pen-yr-Orsedd Quarry was an open working developed from a number of hillside galleries. It was connected to the horse-worked 3ft 6ins gauge Nantlle Tramway and used 1ft 11ins track within the quarry complex. The site was visited only once, in the summer of 1961, when the quarry was on annual holiday. Although slate was still being worked, the scene within the quarry environs was one of utter dereliction; many buildings were in a state of collapse, indeed some had collapsed. The remnants of the Nantlle Tramway, owned by BR and operating from the bottom of the quarry inclines to the standard gauge connection at Nantlle, was still in operation, though in a much run-down state.

❀

Plate 106 – On 26th July 1961, at the upper level of the quarry, several locomotives were in store and clearly had not worked for some years. Peering from the innards of a shed, which was collapsing around it, was *Britomart*, a Hunslet locomotive which, very surprisingly retained its brass name and builder's plates. The plate recorded a works No. 707 and a build date of 1899. Whilst the engine appeared complete and all brass fittings seemed intact, a thick layer of masonry dust covered everything. Happily, *Britomart* was saved for preservation and currently resides on the Festiniog Railway.

Plate 107 – Parked behind *Britomart* was *Una*, another Hunslet locomotive which was in a similar condition, and again complete with name and builder's plates. The shot was taken to record the existence of the second engine as well as to demonstrate the state of the building. Part of the roof had fallen in and one main wall, on the left, had fallen outwards. *Una* was built as Hunslet works No. 873 in 1905 and carried a tool box on top of her saddle tank, which can just be seen in the shot. Happily, *Una*, now owned by the National Museum of Wales, survives in preservation and is based at Gilfach Ddu workshops at Llanberis.

Plate 108 – In another run down building was Kerr, Stuart 'Sirdar' Class 0-4-0 tank locomotive *Diana*, in a very poor state, with some brass fittings missing. Again, the number plates were in place, these indicating a build date of 1917 and works number 1158. *Diana* initially worked on the Kerry Tramway, near Newtown in mid-Wales, and was sold to the Oakley Quarries at Blaenau Festiniog in 1925, from whom it was purchased by Pen-yr-Orsedd in 1945. The engine is currently in private hands and is being restored.

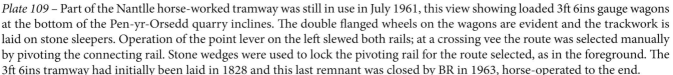

Plate 109 – Part of the Nantlle horse-worked tramway was still in use in July 1961, this view showing loaded 3ft 6ins gauge wagons at the bottom of the Pen-yr-Orsedd quarry inclines. The double flanged wheels on the wagons are evident and the trackwork is laid on stone sleepers. Operation of the point lever on the left slewed both rails; at a crossing vee the route was selected manually by pivoting the connecting rail. Stone wedges were used to lock the pivoting rail for the route selected, as in the foreground. The 3ft 6ins tramway had initially been laid in 1828 and this last remnant was closed by BR in 1963, horse-operated to the end.

❀ *Penrhyn Quarry Railway* ❀

No visit to North Wales railways in the 1950s and early 1960s would have been complete without calling at Coed-y-Parc, Bethesda, the workshops of the Penrhyn Railway. The railway had been built to carry slate from the Penrhyn Quarries to Port Penrhyn on the Menai Straits. Laid to a gauge of 1ft 11ins, the main line was opened in 1879 and ceased operation in 1962. Steam haulage on the quarry tramways continued until 1965.

❀

Plate 110 – One of the first visits to Bethesda was in August 1954, when unfortunately the quarries were closed for the annual holiday and no steam locomotives were working. However, the larger Hunslet 0-4-0ST *Lilla* was in the shed. Built in 1891 for the nearby Cilgwyn Quarry at Nantlle, *Lilla* was bought by Penrhyn Quarries in 1928. Purchased for use on the main line, *Lilla* was taken out of service for boiler repairs in 1955, no further work being undertaken prior to her sale in 1963. Happily returned to working condition in 1996, *Lilla* currently resides on the Festiniog Railway.

Coed-y-Parc
August 1954

Plate 111 – Parked in a cramped corner of the locomotive shed on 5th August 1954 was Avonside Engine Co. No. 2067 *Marchlyn*. Built in 1933, *Marchlyn* was acquired by Penrhyn Quarries in 1936 and sold in 1965; the engine was shipped to the USA that year, where it remains.

Plate 112 – Within the main engine shed at Coed-y-Parc, a very clean 0-4-0ST, *Sybil Mary*, was photographed. Built by Hunslet at Leeds in 1906, this engine was laid up in 1955 with boiler and firebox problems and was sold incomplete in 1965. Whilst now in private hands, *Sybil Mary* remains un-restored.

Plate 113 – On that same August day, 0-4-0ST *Pamela*, built by Hunslet in 1906 and delivered from Leeds at the same time as *Sybil Mary*, was at rest in the shed. Rebuilt in the early 1950s using the boiler from a Hudswell Clarke engine, *Pamela* had a radically altered appearance from her as-built condition. Sold incomplete in 1966, *Pamela* remains un-restored.

Plate 114 – In traditional pose on 17th July 1962, framed by the Coed-y-Parc works doorway, the upper view shows *Blanche*, a Hunslet product of 1893, which had been in the works for minor repairs. The locomotive is exceptionally clean, as evidenced by the condition of the paintwork and lining on the cab and tank panels shown in the lower view (*Plate 115*). At this time the engine was steam braked only and right-hand drive. The very last steam trip over the Penrhyn main line ten days later, on 27th July, would be worked by *Blanche*, which may explain her pristine condition.

Plates 116 and 117 – Still at work in the slate galleries high above Bethesda, Hunslet No. 364 *Winifred* was supplied new to Penrhyn Quarries in 1885. When captured in steam (*above*) on 17th July 1961, the locomotive seemed in excellent condition and was sold in working order in July 1965, the boiler having been fitted with a new firebox in 1953. Resold to owners in the USA, *Winifred* is believed to be in storage and not accessible to the public. On the same visit, Avonside Engine Co. No. 2066 of 1933, *Ogwen* (*lower view*), was also at work shunting spoil wagons to a tip. *Ogwen* also currently resides in the USA.

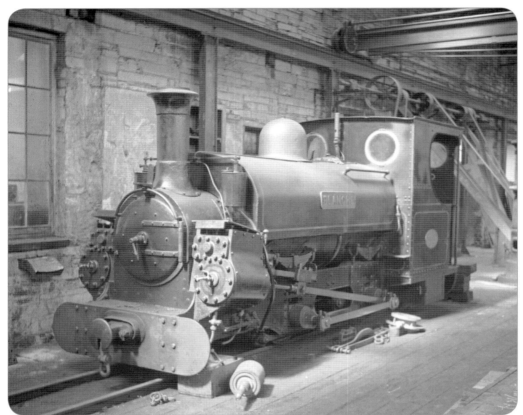

Plate 118 – Almost a year later, on 2nd July 1963, *Blanche* was again recorded at Coed-y-Parc works, having seen very little work on Penrhyn metals over the previous twelve months. On this occasion the locomotive is undergoing a valve examination, and this may relate to her being purchased by the Festiniog Railway in late 1963. Above the cab is the workshop 1-ton hand operated overhead travelling crane and the line shaft from which unguarded belt drives provided power to various machine tools – truly a Victorian scene!

Victorian-style machinery still being used at Coed-y-Parc

Plate 119 – In Coed-y-Parc works on 4th June 1962, Barclay 0-4-0 *Cegin* was undergoing a heavy repair. Built in 1931, *Cegin* was bought by Penrhyn Quarries in 1936. The locomotive was sold as an operational unit in 1965 and is currently in the USA.

Plate 120 – The last locomotive to be overhauled at Coed-y-Parc was Barclay-built *Glyder*, which was photographed whilst undergoing the work on 20th July 1964. Built in 1931, *Glyder* was acquired by Penrhyn in 1936 and sold in 1965. The engine is currently in the USA.

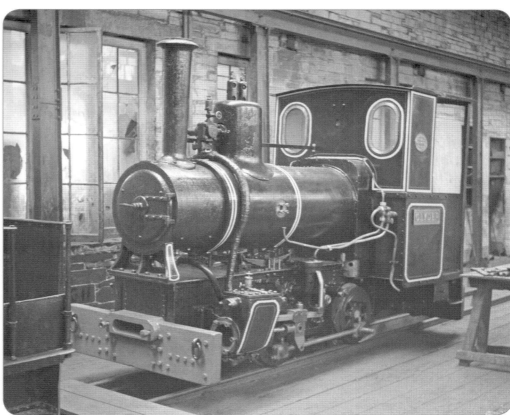

Plate 121 – Having been repaired and repainted, Hunslet No. 704 *Nesta* was in excellent condition in the works on 20th July 1964 prior to being offered for sale. The engine, built in 1899, was acquired by US interests and shipped to the USA with other ex-Penrhyn locomotives in 1965. Sadly, its present whereabouts are unknown.

Plates 122 and 123 – On a dull 2nd July 1962, Barclay No. 1994 *Glyder* was operating in the upper slate galleries. Built at Kilmarnock in 1931 for Durham County Water Board, *Glyder* was acquired by Penrhyn Quarries in 1936. The precarious state of the permanent way and pointwork casts grave doubt on their ability to retain the locomotive and wagon on the track, though double flanges on the wagon wheels should assist. Not surprisingly, the externally mounted regulator valve on these Barclay engines was much preferred to the Hunslet dome-mounted sliding face type.

An altogether more depressing scene awaited visitors to Coed-y-Parc on 27th June 1960. Complete with brass name and builder's plates still fitted but coupling rods missing (they were sold to the Festiniog Railway), *Lilla* indeed looks a sorry sight. Compared to the 1954 visit, when *Lilla* was operational, several years of exposure to the elements has taken its toll (*Plate 124 above*). One might have imagined that things could not get worse but they did! Three years later (*Plate 125 below*) on 2nd July 1963 *Lilla* has decayed further, as evidenced by the state of the smokebox door. Fortunately the builder's plates and many bronze fittings have been removed for safe keeping. Happily, *Lilla* was saved for preservation shortly thereafter, was extensively rebuilt and currently operates on the Festiniog Railway.

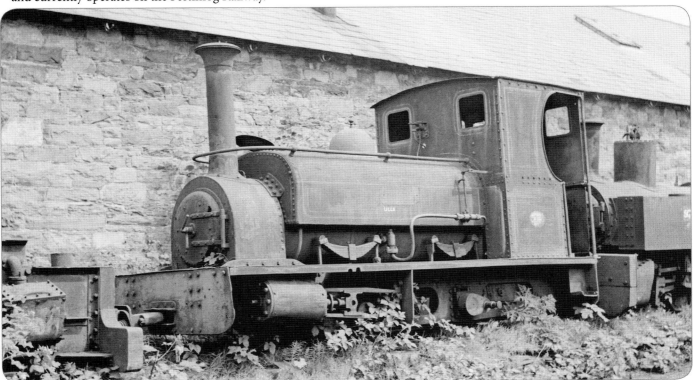

Plate 126 (above) – Also in the scrap line in June 1960 were Orenstein & Koppel 0-4-0 *Eigiau*, bought in 1928, and Kerr, Stuart 0-4-2 *Stanhope*, bought in 1934. Both locomotives were acquired second hand and were in a sorry state after several years in the open, although both still retained their name and builders' plates.

Plate 127 (below) – The remains of *Sgt. Murphy*, built by Kerr, Stuart & Co. for the War Dept as works No. 3117 in 1918, suggested that the locomotive was unlikely ever to turn a wheel again. Purchased second hand and un-named in 1921, it was named by the Penrhyn Quarry authorities after a famous contemporary hurdler, whose gait was said to resemble the engine's motion on the track. *Sgt. Murphy* was the first six-coupled engine at Penrhyn. A major rebuild was undertaken in 1932 and the boiler lowered after a fatal overturning, though by 1955 the firebox was condemned. Happily, the engine was preserved and rebuilt as an 0-6-2T; it re-entered service on the Festiniog Railway in 1993 and now operates on the Teifi Valley Railway.

Plate 128 (above) – Continuing the depressing tendencies, Hunslet No. 317 *Lilian*, built in 1883, was in the scrap line at Coed-y-Parc in June 1960. Again, quite surprisingly, the locomotive which had lain in this condition for over three years retains its brass name and builder's plates as well as many bronze fittings. Fortunately, the engine was purchased in 1965 and restored to full running order, now operating at the Launceston Steam Railway.

Plate 129 (below) – On the same day in 1960, Manning Wardle No. 1382 of 1897, whilst more complete than *Lilla*, was nevertheless in a distressed state, having been withdrawn from service in 1955 with boiler problems. Named *Jubilee 1897*, for obvious reasons, the locomotive had, like *Lilla*, been acquired from Cilgwyn Quarries in 1928. No longer operational, the locomotive was cosmetically restored and resides in the Narrow Gauge Railway Museum at Towyn.

Plate 130 – After the depressing sights of the Coed-y-Parc scrap road, an altogether more pleasing vista was provided on 26th June 1960 by main line Hunslet No. 590 *Linda* of 1893, which was under repair. The locomotive was clean and in excellent mechanical condition, connecting rod bearing bushes being given attention. *Linda* made her last journey on the Penrhyn Railway in July 1962, after which she was hired to the Festiniog Railway, who purchased the engine outright in 1963. In 1960, *Linda* was steam braked only and right hand drive.

On a sunny 2nd July 1962, Avonside Engine Co. 0-4-0 *Ogwen* was in steam among the galleries. Built for Durham County Water Board in 1933, *Ogwen* was acquired by Penrhyn Quarries in 1936 and was the last steam locomotive operating in the quarries when steam traction ceased in January 1965. The engine is currently in the USA. In the upper view (*Plate 131*), the galleries in the background stretch the whole way round the hillside, there being at least seven discrete levels visible. The double flanged wheels on the steel-sided slate wagons are most obvious. The slate cutting sheds with their individual rail tracks figure prominently in the lower photograph (*Plate 132*).

❀ *Snowdon Mountain Railway* ❀

Several trips were made with the family on this famous railway, which was opened in 1896 and which operates using the Abt rack system, patented in 1882 by a Swiss engineer, Dr Roman Abt. In fine weather, unrivalled panoramic views of the surrounding countryside can be seen from the Snowdon summit at 3,650ft. All the steam locomotives supplied to the railway were built by SLM at Winterthur, Switzerland.

At the Llanberis terminus, engines are prepared for the journey to the summit and two of the special locomotives were captured there on 3rd August 1954. No. 5 *Moel Siabod* (*Plate 133 above*) is one of the earlier types, built in Switzerland in 1896; currently this engine is out of traffic awaiting boiler repairs. No. 6 *Padarn* (*Plate 134 left*), an SLM product of 1922, is currently in service. When entering SMR service in 1923, No. 6 was named *Sir Harmood* after Sir Harmood Banner, the first chairman of the Snowdon Mountain Tramroad & Hotel Co. Ltd.

Plate 135 – Built in 1895, No. 3 *Wyddfa* is one of the original locomotives ordered from SML for the opening in 1896. On 12th June 1960, No. 3, which is still in service, waits her next duty in the locomotive shed yard at Llanberis.

Plate 136 (below) – On 10th June 1962, No. 7 *Aylwin* waits at Llanberis while passengers board the next summit-bound train. *Aylwin*, built by SLM in 1923, is no longer in service.

On the rack …

Plate 137 – Keeping the SMR special steam locomotives in tip-top condition is a vital part of SMR every day business. Workshops at Llanberis undertake ongoing maintenance work and major overhauls, as evidenced by No. 5 *Moel Siabod* undergoing boiler re-staying work on 11th July 1963.

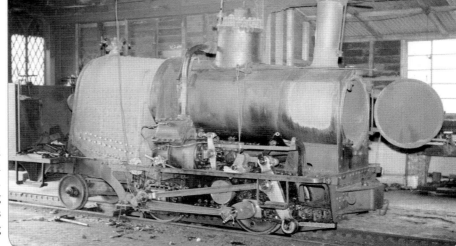

Plate 138 – On a very misty 3rd August 1954, a train enters the summit station; on this occasion very little of the surrounding scenery was visible.

Plate 139 – On 2nd July 1962, No. 8 *Eryri* waits in the station yard to take the next departure for the summit. *Eryri*, which is the Welsh name for Snowdonia, was built by SLM in 1923 and is no longer in service, having been dismantled in the 1980s. As with all SMR trains, there is no fixed coupling between the engine and carriage; this view of No. 8's buffer beam attesting to that.

These two views of SMR locomotives in operation were taken on 17th July 1961 in the vicinity of the upper part of the Afon Hwch Viaduct. In *Plate 140 (above)*, No. 7 *Aylwin*, with steam in hand, descends from the summit. In addition to the safety valves blowing off, the air/water injection braking system is in use, as evidenced by the steam escaping from the vent at the back of the cab. In this system, the locomotive cylinders are used as air compressors and water is injected as a coolant. This braking system converts mechanical energy to compressed air and steam, thereby providing a controllable braking force. In *Plate 141 (below)*, No. 8 *Eryri* pushes its uncoupled carriage to the summit, again with safety valves lifting. Both *Aylwin* and *Eryri* are currently out of service.

❀ *Vale of Rheidol Railway* ❀

With its terminus and locomotive shed at Aberystwyth, the Vale of Rheidol Railway was opened in 1902. The railway was visited several times in the late 1950s and early 1960s. At that time, the VoR had its own station and the engines had their own shed, separate from the standard gauge BR depot. With the closure of Aberystwyth standard gauge depot in the mid-1960s, the VoR took over the redundant shed buildings and the separate VoR station was closed, the VoR trains then having access to the main line station.

Plate 142 – On a sunny 29th July 1958, No. 9 *Prince of Wales* awaits departure from the VoR station at Aberystwyth. Originally built by Davies & Metcalfe in 1902, and numbered 2 by the VoR, No. 9 was initially numbered 1213 by the GWR, and was significantly rebuilt in 1923-24. The evidence of GWR features are obvious: copper capped chimney, bulbous dome cover and brass safety valve bonnet having been substituted for the original fittings during the rebuild. This view shows the engine had no smokebox number plate or shed code plate fitted at July 1958. Happily, *Prince of Wales* still operates on the VoR, which is now run by a charitable trust. The bogie coach coupled to No. 9 is W4148W, built by the GWR in 1938.

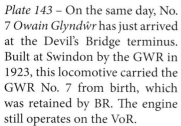

29th July 1958

Plate 143 – On the same day, No. 7 *Owain Glyndŵr* has just arrived at the Devil's Bridge terminus. Built at Swindon by the GWR in 1923, this locomotive carried the GWR No. 7 from birth, which was retained by BR. The engine still operates on the VoR.

Plate 144 – On a rather dull 10th July 1963, No. 9 *Prince of Wales* starts away from the VoR Aberystwyth terminus. To the left of the locomotive are the lines to the VoR shed, which had stand-alone coaling and watering facilities.

At Aberystwyth

Plate 145 – Inside the shed on 15th August 1964 was No. 8 *Llywelyn*, which was built by the GWR at Swindon, and was delivered to Aberystwyth in January 1924. This locomotive, as were its sisters, was fitted with safety chains on both front and rear buffer beams. In 1963, the long time Machynlleth shed code of 89C was changed to 6F as the North Wales area was transferred to the London Midland region, a change to non-Welsh responsibility, which would be unthinkable today.

Plate 146 – From the retaining wall, which bounded one side of the locomotive depot, the pedigree of No. 8 *Llywelyn* is immediately obvious. The copper chimney cap, the dome cover form and safety valve casing all point to a Swindon conception. This photograph was taken on 14th July 1964.

Plate 147 - Even in GWR days, the VoR had little need of freight wagons. Two cattle trucks were built by the GWR at Swindon for the VoR in 1923 but were unused for many years and subsequently re-gauged in 1937 for use on the Welshpool & Llanfair Light Railway (also owned by the GWR). Locomotive coal wagons were needed, however, since coal was obtained from the main line depot as required. On 20th July 1958, two such wagons were parked at the VoR running shed. No's W34141 and W34136 had end doors, were hand braked only and fitted with safety chains.

❀ *Talyllyn Railway* ❀

The Talyllyn Railway was completed in 1865, to a gauge of 2ft 3ins, to carry slate from the quarries at Bryn Eglwys to Towyn, for onward shipment by rail. The TR was rescued by a preservation society in 1951 and never actually closed in an operational sense. The railway was visited in both the 1950s and early 1960s. From the time of opening, due to limited clearances, carriage doors could only open on one side, a position that continues today. Also, at the time of the visits, the TR was exempt from railway regulations requiring the use of continuous brakes throughout the train.

Plates 148 and 149 – In 1954, the TR acquired by donation an ex-RAF 0-4-0WT built by Barclay at Kilmarnock in 1918. After re-gauging from 2ft to 2ft 3ins and some rebuilding, No. 6 *Douglas* proved a very capable addition to the TR locomotive fleet. *Douglas*, named after the donor, is seen here in steam at Pendre on a sunny 3rd July 1959.

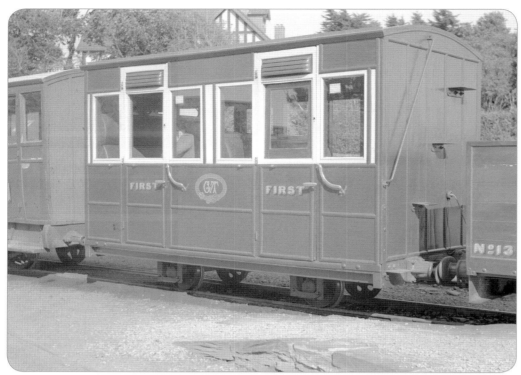

Plate 150 – On 19th July 1959, an ex-Glyn Valley Tramway 4-wheeled coach formed part of a morning train waiting departure from Wharf station. Built for the GVT in 1892, the coach was retrieved by the TR in 1956. After a major refurbishment, it entered TR revenue earning service in 1958, a supplement being charged for First Class travel. To the left is one of the original First Class three-compartment 4-wheeled coaches supplied in 1866 and on the right an open 4-wheeled coach, No. 13.

Plate 151 (below) – Taken on 30th June 1959 at Wharf station, this view shows three of the original TR 4-wheeled coaches. At the left is a First Class three-compartment vehicle; in the centre is a Third Class three-compartment coach: at the right is a brake van, which had been converted to a travelling booking and ticket office. All three coaches were supplied by Brown, Marshalls in 1866 and have no hinged doors at this side, due to clearance restrictions. All brassware and door handles on this side of the train have been removed.

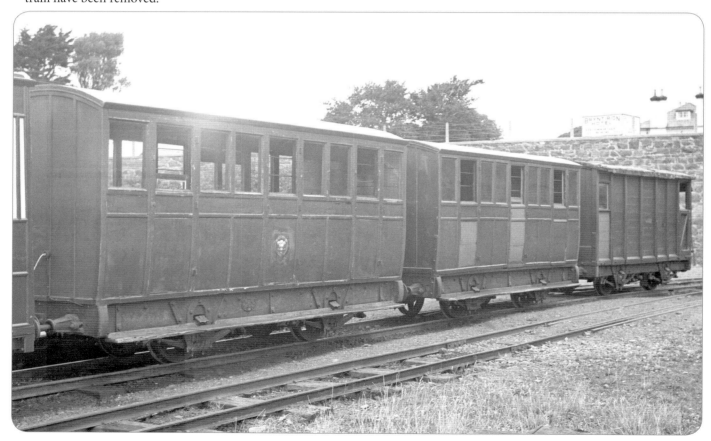

Plate 152 – On 20th July 1959, TR No. 1 *Talyllyn* prepares to leave Wharf station on a morning trip to Abergynolwyn. Built in 1865 for the TR by Fletcher Jennings at Whitehaven, *Talyllyn* had just re-entered service after rebuilding by Gibbons Bros Ltd at Beverly Hill, Staffs and a plate to that effect is affixed to the cab side sheet. The engine remains in service today, 134 years after building. The train has no continuous brake, braking being provided on the locomotive and in the two guards' vans; the one immediately behind the engine is the original Brown, Marshalls 4-wheeled brake van supplied to the TR in 1866.

Plate 153 – In 1951, the TR purchased items of ex-Corris Railway equipment from BR, including an 0-4-2T built in 1878 by Hughes Locomotive & Tramway Co. of Loughborough. Track and wheel gauging problems resulting in derailments on TR tracks severely curtailed the use of this engine for a number of years. Numbered 3 and named *Sir Haydn* by the TR, the locomotive was stored in the old carriage shed at Pendre and was pictured there on 28th June 1959.

Plate 154 – Passing under the road bridge just after departure from Wharf station on 10th July 1959, *Edward Thomas* tackles the gradient heading for Pendre. An ex-Corris Railway 0-4-2T built by Kerr, Stuart in 1921, the engine was acquired by the TR in 1951 from BR and named after Edward Thomas, who had served the TR for over sixty years, latterly as a director. From 1958 to 1969, the locomotive was fitted with a Giesl ejector.

Plate 155 – At Wharf station on 22nd June 1959, TR No. 5 *Midlander* waits to take empty trucks to Pendre. Built by Ruston & Hornsby in 1940 and acquired from Jees' Quarry at Nuneaton, No. 5 continues in service in rebuilt form.

Plate 156 – Awaiting departure from Wharf station with a rake of original TR 4-wheeled coaches on 13th July 1959 is No. 1 *Talyllyn*. The front buffer beam shows the absence of continuous braking pipe work and any safety chains.

Plate 157 – Photographed at Abergynolwyn on 8th July 1959, this is the ex-Corris Railway brake van acquired by the TR in 1951. Built by the Falcon Works at Loughborough in 1878, it was fitted with a new body in 1958, whilst retaining the original wheel sets, and continues in TR service to the present day. To the right of the brake van are original TR Third and First Class 4-wheeled coaches. The brake van and coaches are seen from the side provided with doors.

Plates 158 and 159 - Newly introduced to TR traffic in 1961, an ex-Corris Railway bogie coach is marshalled into a rake of stock at Pendre on a sunny 24th July in that same year. Originally built for the Corris Railway by the Metropolitan Carriage & Wagon Co. in 1898, the carriage was used as a greenhouse and garden shed near Oswestry until recovered by the TR in 1958. The rebuilt body is a replica of the original on a replacement underframe and bogies. On 25th November 1982, the coach carried HRH the Princess of Wales from Pendre to Rhydyronen, the Prince travelling on the footplate of *Dolgoch*.

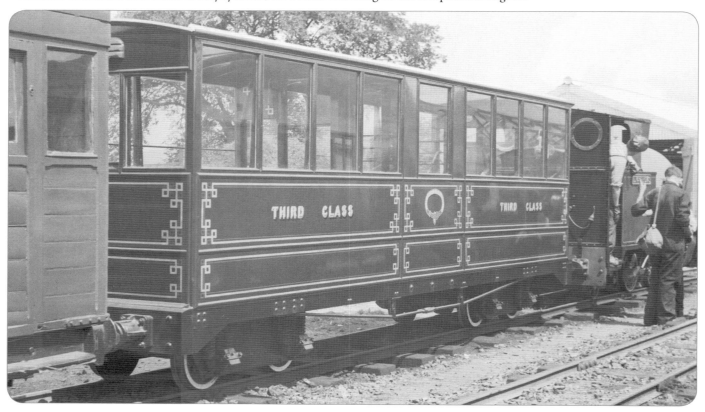

Standing in sunshine at Pendre (*Plate 160, right*) on 17th July 1964, TR No. 2 *Dolgoch* waits to move down to Wharf station. Built by Fletcher Jennings at Whitehaven in 1866 and incorporating Fletcher's patent, No. 2 was the mainstay of passenger train operation in the early years of TR preservation. On the same day No. 1 *Talyllyn* (*Plate 161, below*) waits to depart from Wharf station. The year 1964 was the first of many in which both No. 1 and No. 2 operated together whilst approaching their respective centenaries.

17th July 1964

Plate 162 – On 19th July 1959, ex-Corris Railway 0-4-2T *Edward Thomas* prepares to leave Wharf station. This locomotive, purchased from BR in 1951, underwent repairs by Hunslet at Leeds, and entered TR service in 1952, being fitted with the Giesl ejector shown in this view from 1958 to 1969. A similar Kerr, Stuart 'Tattoo' Class engine, *Stanhope*, has been preserved, after almost fifty years out of use and operates on the West Lancashire Railway.

Plate 163 – Photographed from the last coach, *Talyllyn* heads a heavy train for Towyn at Dolgoch station on 24th July 1961. In the centre of the train are three 4-wheeled, three-compartment open carriages, rebuilt in 1956 using running gear from scrapped Festiniog Railway quarrymen's coaches. In a most relaxed manner, tickets are being inspected and passengers from the open carriages are able to stretch their legs. These open carriages were subsequently rebuilt to unglazed roofed condition.

❀ *The Great Orme Railway* ❀

Built between 1901-04, the 3ft 6ins gauge GOR operates between Llandudno and Great Ormeshead and uses cable haulage to which the cars are permanently attached. Initially operated as a private company, the GOR was acquired by Llandudno UDC in 1949 and continues under local authority ownership. Originally the haulage system was powered by a steam plant located at Half-way station. Equipment similar to colliery winding engines was used until 1957, when electric cable drive was substituted for steam. My family's first visit to the GOR was in 1954, in the era of steam-powered haulage.

Plate 164 – On 28th July 1954 car No. 7 waits at the summit as passengers board for the return trip to Llandudno. The four operating cars No's 4-7 were built in 1902-03 by Hurst, Nelson & Co. of Motherwell, Scotland, then a well established tramcar builder.

❀

Plate 165 – On the same day, car No. 4 descends past the half-way point. In 1932, this car was involved in a major accident when, due to metal fatigue, the car drawbar became detached from the haulage cable. In the subsequent runaway on the steep 1 in 3.7 stretch at Tabor Hill the car left the rails and crashed into a wall with fatal consequences.

28th July 1954

Plate 166 – In this view taken from the driver's platform of the descending vehicle, car No. 5 makes its way to the summit at the passing point. The trolley poles fitted to the car roofs are not associated with power transmission but were provided to allow a telephone link between the driver and the winding house.

❁ *South of Portmadoc – British Railways* ❁

Whilst holidaying in North Wales, occasional forays were made to the central Wales coastal resorts, particularly Aberystwyth and also to Machynlleth. In steam days, Machynlleth was a sizeable depot providing motive power for through routes including South Wales, via Moat Lane. Most unfortunately, the Beeching cuts significantly reduced the central Wales rail network.

Plate 167 – On a wet and dull 24th June 1959, BR-built pannier tank No. 1636 awaits its next duty at Machynlleth shed. Built at Swindon in 1951, No. 1636 would survive for another five years, being withdrawn in 1964 from Didcot. One has to question the building of such locomotives in the early 1950s, when 350hp diesel shunters were readily available.

❁

Plate 168 – On the same day at Machynlleth, ex-GWR '1400' Class 0-4-2T No. 5809 was resting between turns, though coaled and ready for the road. Built at Swindon in 1933, No. 5809 would be withdrawn two months later in August 1959 and scrapped at Swindon.

Plate 169 (*above*) – Ex-GWR 'Manor' Class locomotives were the mainstay of express passenger services on Cambrian lines in the 1950s and, on 23rd July 1959, No. 7819 *Hinton Manor* and No. 7810 *Draycott Manor* were in steam at Aberystwyth shed awaiting their next passenger turns. Built at Swindon in 1939, *Hinton Manor*, which was withdrawn in 1965, survives in preservation on the Severn Valley Railway. The less fortunate *Draycott Manor*, built at Swindon in 1938, was withdrawn from Machynlleth in 1964 and scrapped.

Plate 170 (*below*) – BR-built 'Manor' Class locomotive No. 7821 *Ditcheat Manor* was being prepared at Aberystwyth for its next passenger duty on 28th July 1964. By this time, Machynlleth depot had been transferred to the London Midland region of BR and the engine sports a 6F shedplate. The crosshead driven vacuum pump fitted under the running board is prominent. Built at Swindon in 1950, No. 7821 would be withdrawn in 1965 prior to preservation at the West Somerset Railway.

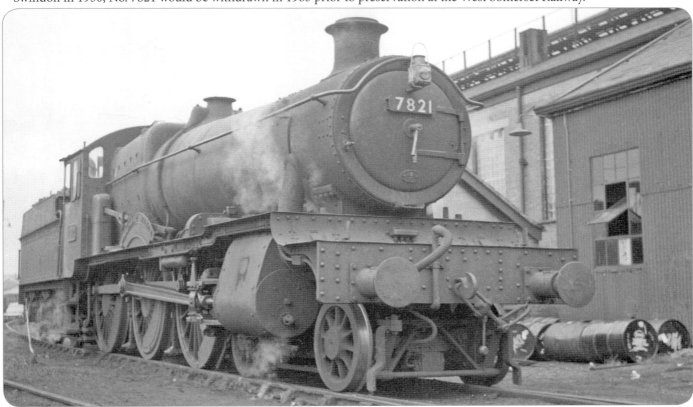

Plate 171 – Also at Machynlleth on 24th June 1959, ex-GWR 'Dukedog' 4-4-0 No. 9018, was coaled and awaiting its next duty. Built at Swindon in 1938 using Bulldog frames, No. 9018 was withdrawn in 1960 from Croes Newydd. Although allocated the name *Earl of Birkenhead*, the nameplate was never carried by this engine. No. 9017 of this class is preserved on the Bluebell Railway.

Plate 172 – Goods traffic on the Cambrian coast lines was still a significant part of railway business even in the early 1960s. On 17th June 1961, BR Class '2MT' No. 78006 and an unidentified ex-GWR pannier tank double-head a goods working heading south from Towyn goods yard. This view was taken from the Talyllyn Railway loading dock, then served by a BR siding. The '2MT' was built at Darlington in 1953 and withdrawn in 1965.

Plate 173 – At Aberystwyth, ex-GWR '7400' Class pannier tank No. 7417 was acting as shed pilot. Built at Swindon in 1937, No. 7417 was withdrawn from Machynlleth in 1961.

Aberystwyth, 19th July 1959

Plate 174 - Same day, same place, ex-GWR '4300' Class 'Mogul' No. 6371 was receiving attention from its driver prior to departure from the shed. Built in 1921 by Robert Stephenson and Co., No. 6371 was withdrawn in September 1960 and scrapped at Swindon after a creditable thirty-nine years service.

Plate 175 – On 16th June 1960, ex-GWR 'Manor' Class No. 7819 *Hinton Manor* is being coaled at Aberystwyth main line shed, prior to its next turn. Built at Swindon in 1939, No. 7819 survives in preservation and operates on the Severn Valley Railway.

Plate 176 – At Towyn station on 19th July 1958, ex-GWR '4500' Class No. 5565 awaits departure for the south on a passenger working. Built at Swindon in 1929, No. 5565 would be withdrawn in September 1960.

Plate 177 – On a dull and wet 22nd June 1959, ex-GWR 2-6-2T No. 5541 rests between duties at Machynlleth. Built at Swindon in 1928, No. 5541 would spend over twenty years in service allocated to 89C, Machynlleth. The engine would survive for another three years prior to withdrawal from Laira in July 1962, having run over 900,000 miles in thirty-four years service. Sold to Woodham Bros at Barry later that year, No. 5541 would lie at Barry for ten years until purchased in 1972 by the Dean Forest Railway, where it has been restored to working condition.

A final glimpse: Welsh narrow gauge with British Railways overtones, 27th July 1959

Travelling through the Rheidol Valley in the 1950s, when far fewer road vehicles were around, was a delightful experience. *Plate 178 (above)* shows Vale of Rheidol No. 9 *Prince of Wales* climbing hard through the valley, whilst *Plate 179 (below)* is of the same engine coasting downhill towards Aberystwyth. The pictures were taken from an open sided coach, affording spectacular views.